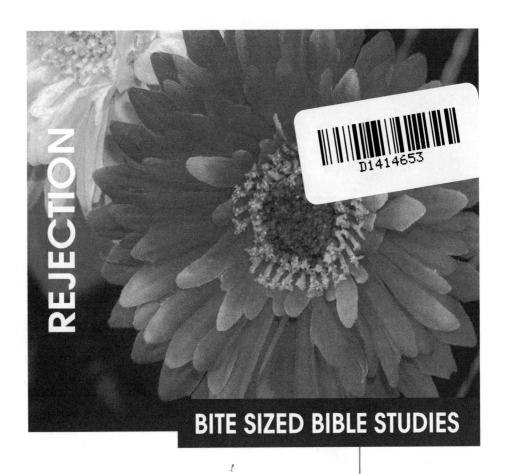

REJECTION

BITE SIZED BIBLE STUDIES

Kissed *Or* Dissed

God's Word For
Feeling Rejected & Overlooked

6 SESSIONS

BETH JONES

When your words came, I ate them;
they were my joy and my heart's delight . . .
Jeremiah 15:16 NIV

The Bite Sized Bible Study Series Includes . . .

- Satisfied Lives For Desperate Housewives: God's Word On Proverbs 31
- Kissed or Dissed: God's Word For Feeling Rejected & Overlooked
- Grace For The Pace: God's Word For Stressed & Overloaded Lives
- Don't Factor Fear Here: God's Word For Overcoming Anxiety, Fear & Phobias
- The Friends God Sends: God's Word On Friendship & Chick Chat
- What To Do When You Feel Blue: God's Word For Depression & Discouragement

Beth Jones is a Bible teacher, author, wife and mother of four children who ministers the Word of God in a relevant and inspiring way by sharing down-to-earth insights. She is the author of the popular Bible study series *Getting A Grip On The Basis* which is being used by thousands of churches in America and abroad, *Why The Gory, Bloody Details?*, and the *Bite Sized Bible Study Series.* Beth also writes a bi-weekly newspaper column titled *"Just Us Girls"* and hosts www.bethjones.org. She and her husband Jeff founded and serve as the senior pastors of Kalamazoo Valley Family Church.

Beth Jones may be reached @
Kalamazoo Valley Family Church, 269.324.5599
www.bethjones.org or www.kvfc.org

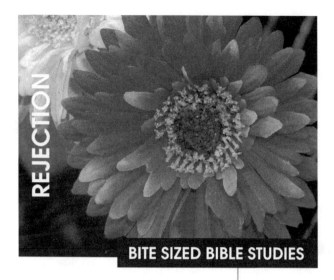

REJECTION

BITE SIZED BIBLE STUDIES

Kissed *Or* Dissed

God's Word For
Feeling Rejected & Overlooked

6 SESSIONS

BETH JONES

VALLEY PRESS
PUBLISHERS

Valley Press Publishers

Portage, MI

valleypresspublishers.com

Kissed Or Dissed
God's Word For Rejection & Feeling Overlooked
ISBN: 1-933433-01-9

Copyright © 2005 Beth Ann Jones

Published by Valley Press Publishers - A Ministry of KVFC
995 Romence Road, Portage, MI 49024
800-596-0379   www.kvfc.org

Printed in the United States of America.
ALL RIGHTS RESERVED.

For information: Please contact Valley Press Publishers.

All Scripture quotations are taken from The King James Bible,
unless otherwise noted.

Scripture quotations marked (AMP) are taken from the Amplified Bible, Copyright © 1954, 1958, 1962, 1964, 1965, 1987 by the Lockman Foundation. Used by permission.

Scripture quotations marked (NLT) are taken from the Holy Bible, New Living Translation, Copyright © 1996. Used by permission of Tyndale House Publishers, Inc., Wheaton, Illinois 60189. All rights reserved.

Scripture quotations marked (NKJV) are taken from the New King James Version. Copyright © 1982 by Thomas Nelson, Inc. Used by permission. All rights reserved.

Scripture quotations marked (NIV) are taken from the HOLY BIBLE, NEW INTERNATIONAL VERSION®, NIV®. Copyright © 1973, 1978, 1984 by International Bible Society. Used by permission of Zondervan. All rights reserved.

The Message: Scripture quotations marked (The Message) are taken from *The Message* by Eugene H. Peterson, Copyright © 1993, 1994, 1995, 1996, 2000, 2001, 2002. Used by permission of NavPress Publishing Group. All rights reserved.

Scripture quotations marked (TLB) are taken from The Living Bible, Copyright © 1971. Used by permission of Tyndale House Publishers, Inc., Wheaton, Illinois 60189. All rights reserved.

Contents

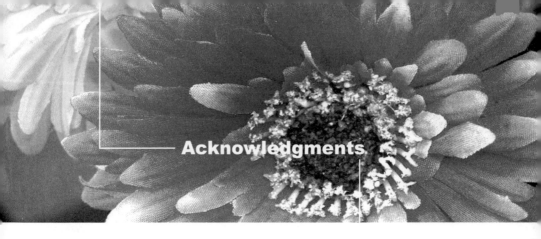

Acknowledgments

Writing a book is like having a baby! I've been "pregnant" with many books over the years and have found that once a book is "conceived" by the Holy Spirit and begins to grow, the gestation period can range from a few years to several decades. Then it seems that at the right time, when I'm "full-term" and "great with child", the Lord puts an "urge" to write within me which eventually triggers the labor pains, transition and ultimately the birth of a book! It takes a lot of people to give birth to a book and I'd like to honor those the Lord has put in my life to coach, pray, support and encourage me in these writing endeavors.

First, my husband, Jeff. You have been my best friend and most consistent encourager. When I have been uncertain, you've always been rock solid and gone the extra mile to help me fulfill God's will in writing. Thanks for loving me and believing in God's call on my life.

Second, my children, Meghan, Annie, Luke and Eric. I've had to take more time away to write; thanks for being understanding and willing to let mom go. I couldn't have asked for four better children. I love you all.

Third, my mom. What an inspiration you have always been to me! Thanks for letting me hang out with you in Florida to write these books.

Fourth, our staff. Our Associate Publisher, April Wedel, our Editorial Coordinator, Juli DeGraaf and our Publications Coordinator, Joanne Davis. I appreciate your love, faith, heart to get the Word out and the long hours you have spent helping me give birth to this book! I also want to thank the entire KVFC staff for their love, support and encouragement.

Fifth, all the volunteer copy editors and pray-ers. A very special thanks to Mary VanderWal, Carol Lacey and Elise Burch for your time, comments and editing help. I especially appreciate my dear praying friends Mary VanderWal, Mary Jo Fox, Kate Cook, Cindy Boester, Jennifer Nederhoed, Pam Roe-Vanderberg, Jennifer Palthe, Colleen DeBruin, Molly Nicolai, KVFC prayer teams and many others who have continually lifted me and these projects to the Lord in prayer.

Sixth, Pat Judd, Bryan Norris and all the guys with CrossStaff. Thanks for partnering with us in this project. Let's have fun watching what the Lord will do!

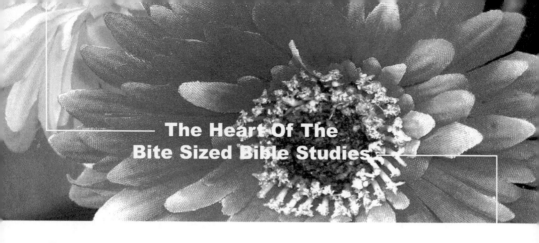

I love God's Word. I don't just like it; I love it. It's more valuable to me than anything. If I had to spend the rest of my life on a remote, uninhabited island and could only take one thing, I would take my Bible. Why? It's simple. God has changed and upgraded every area of my life as I have simply read, believed and obeyed the Bible.

It wasn't always that way. Like many people, I had never even considered reading the Bible for myself, much less studying it. The Bible was for priests, theologians and monks. It was not relevant to my life. It was a dusty old book in our basement. One day, when I was about 14 years old, I just got the "urge" to read the Bible. I started with Genesis, and within the first few chapters I fell asleep. That was the end of my Bible reading.

It wasn't until five years later when I was a 19-year-old college freshman that my roommate began to share with me what the Bible said about God, about life and about me. I was shocked at the "living" quality of the Bible. It wasn't like any other book I read. This wasn't like reading the president's biography. This wasn't like reading the dull Western Civilization textbooks in front of me. It was as if God Himself was explaining the contents to me. Something was happening in my heart as I read God's Word. I was challenged. I was encouraged. I was comforted. The Living God was speaking through His Living Word. During this time I developed a hunger for God and His Word. I stayed up late to read the Bible. I pondered it during the day. There was plenty I didn't understand, but I received strength, energy and wisdom just by reading it, and ultimately the Holy Spirit drew me to Jesus.

As a new Christian in my sophomore year of college, my Bible study leader simply exhorted me to read my Bible a lot and "let the Word of Christ dwell richly inside of me." It was the best advice ever! The result was that I began to develop an insatiable appetite for God's Word and a passionate desire to share God's Word with others. As I read my Bible, Jesus walked off the pages and came to live in my heart. Jesus isn't just alive in heaven, He is alive to me. I've come to know Him intimately through fellowship with Him in His Word.

Isn't it great that God's Word is interactive—not just historic or static? God's Word is living and active and able to effectually work within us to affect change and impart the miraculous! The Bible is the most amazing book ever! It has been banned, burned and blasted, but it lives on and continues to be the world's best-selling book.

Unfortunately, I have found that lots of people just don't understand the Bible and as a result, they get overwhelmed, bored or frustrated. Many Christians have never really tasted the rich, daily, life-changing flavor of God's Word. If you want to grow and mature in God, you have to "eat" large quantities of the Word. Once you taste and see that the Lord and His Word are good, nothing else will satisfy you! Think of it this way: if all you've ever tasted are peanut butter and jelly sandwiches, then you are pretty content with a good PBJ. But the minute you taste a filet mignon, you can never again be satisfied by a PBJ. In some ways, I have found that is the story for many Christians. If you're one of those people that have been content with a spiritual PBJ, I've got good news for you; get your taste buds ready for some rich, tasty, "meaty" morsels from God's Word. The more you eat it, the better it tastes!

Our goal in the Bite Sized Bible Study Series is to create an addiction in you for Bible study, and more importantly for knowing God intimately through the revelation knowledge of His Word, by His Spirit. As you explore these studies, I believe that the Holy Spirit will speak to your heart and transmit the supernatural revelation you need to operate victoriously in this life.

Jeremiah was right:

"When your words came, I ate them;
they were my joy and my heart's delight . . ."
Jeremiah 15:16, NIV

May this be your testimony, too!

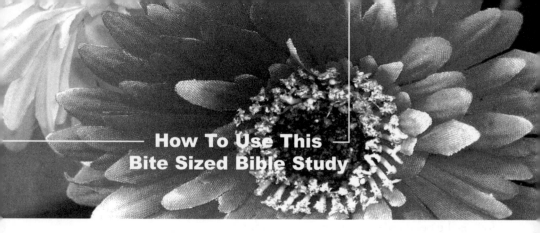

How To Use This Bite Sized Bible Study

This Bible study can be used individually as well as in small groups. It's ideal for those who are hungry to learn from the Word, but who have a limited amount of time to meet together with others.

The Bite Sized Bible Study Series is designed for all types of Bible study formats.

* Individual Study
* Women's Small Groups
* Lunchtime Study at Work
* Neighborhood Bible Study
* Couples' Small Groups
* Sunday School Class
* Prison Ministry
* Student and Youth Small Groups
* Outreach Bible Study
* Early Morning Men's Bible Groups
* Singles Small Groups
* Recovery and Felt Need Groups

For Individual Study

Pray. Ask God, by the Holy Spirit, to customize these sessions for you personally.

Expect. Turn your "expectation" on and trust God to speak to your heart.

Dive. Grab your Bible, pen and favorite beverage and dive in!

For Small Group Study Leaders

Pray. Ask God, by the Holy Spirit, to reveal and customize these sessions for you and your group members.

Expect. Turn your "expectation" on and trust God to speak to your heart, as well as the hearts of those in your small group.

Facilitate. Small groups will do better with a facilitator, preferably a more mature Christian who can add helpful comments as well as lead a heartfelt time of prayer before and after each session. It's important that you keep things moving in the right direction. As the leader of the small group, keep in mind that it's your job to facilitate discussion and not act as the "teacher" who does all the talking. It's important for those in the group to verbalize their discoveries, so do your best to create an atmosphere where each member feels free to share what they are learning from God's Word.

Encourage. Encourage everyone to participate. Help those who talk a lot to take a breather and let others share their insights as well.

Focus. Stay focused on God the Father, Jesus, and the Holy Spirit Who gave us the Scriptures. Our goal is to see what God has said in His Word. Keep in mind that this is a Bible study and not a place for "my opinion" or "my church believes" or "here's what I think" comments. Always direct people's attention back to the Bible to see what the Scriptures say.

Highlight. Hit the high points. If you face time constraints, you may not have enough time to cover every detail of each lesson. As the leader, prayerfully prepare and be sure you cover the highlights of each session.

Digest. We've endeavored to "cut up" the Word through this Bite Sized Bible Study, and as a leader it's your job to help those in your small group digest the Scriptures so they can benefit from all the spiritual nutrition in each word.

Discuss. Take time to answer the three discussion questions at the end of each Bible study session. These should help stimulate heartfelt conversation.

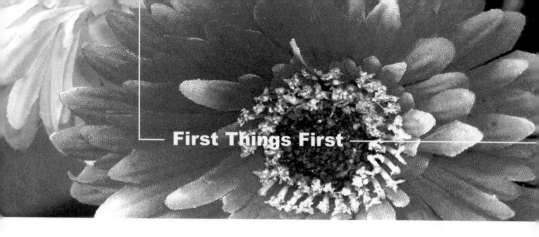

If you want this Bible study to really impact your life, you must be certain of one major thing: you must be certain you are a Christian according to God's definition and instruction in the Bible. You must be certain that you are accepted by God; that you are saved. So let's begin our study by considering this important issue.

Did you know that some people want to be a Christian on their terms, rather than on God's terms? Sometimes people want to emphasize church, religion and their goodness as evidence of their Christianity. For some, it will be a rude awakening to discover that the Bible tells us God isn't impressed by any of those substitutes. Did you know that God isn't interested in our denominational tags? He's not wowed by our church membership pedigree, either. He's not moved by our good deeds and benevolent accomplishments. The thing that most impresses God is His Son, Jesus Christ. *"For God so loved the world that he gave his one and only Son, that whoever believes in him shall not perish but have eternal life." John 3:16, NIV* God paid quite a price to send His own Son to the cross to pay the penalty for our sin. It's really an insult to Him to trust in or substitute anything or anyone else for Jesus Christ. The key to being a Christian is to believe in, trust, receive and confess Jesus Christ as your Lord and Savior.

Why would you or anyone want to believe in, trust, receive and confess Jesus Christ as Lord? Why would you want to know Jesus personally and to be known by Him? Unless you truly understand your condition before God, you wouldn't have any reason to! However, when you realize the magnitude of your sin—those private and public thoughts, deeds, actions and words that you and God know about—when you listen to your conscience and realize that truly "all have sinned," including you, it can be very sobering. It's even more sobering to realize that according to God's justice system, *". . . the wages of sin is death . . ." Romans 6:23 NKJV* It's a big wake up call when it really hits you that the consequence of sin is death. Death which is defined as an eternal separation from God is the payment you will receive for your sin. When you realize your true, hopeless, lost condition before God, you will run to Him in order to be saved. This reality causes people to quit playing religious games and to quit trusting in their own works of righteousness. Our lost condition forces us to forgo being "churchy" or "religious", apathetic, passive and indifferent, and to become hungry for the Merciful Living God. It's good news to discover that " . . . *the gift of God is eternal life in Christ Jesus our Lord." Romans 6:23 NKJV*

What does God require of us? The qualification for eternal life is simply to believe on Jesus. Many people say they believe in God or in Jesus Christ. In fact, the Bible tells us that the devil himself believes and trembles. According to the Bible, God's definition of a Christian believer—or a Christ One—is the person who believes in their heart that God raised Jesus from the dead and who confesses with his or her mouth that Jesus Christ is their Lord. In other words, their heart and mouth agree that Jesus is Lord! We see this in Romans 10:13, 9, ". . . *whoever calls on the name of the LORD shall be saved . . . if you confess with your mouth the Lord Jesus and believe in your heart that God has raised Him from the dead, you will be saved." NKJV*

This is something we do on purpose. It's a sobering thought to consider that if you've never purposely repented of your sin and invited Jesus Christ to be the Lord of your life, you may not be saved—you may not be a Christian according to God's definition. Would you like to be certain that you are a Christian; that you have a relationship with the Lord and eternal salvation? It's simple, just answer these questions: Do you believe that God raised Jesus from the dead? Will you give Him the steering wheel of your life and trust Him to forgive all your sins and make you an entirely new person? Will you trust Jesus Christ alone to save you? Are you willing to invite Him into your life and will you confess that He is your Lord? If so, please pray this prayer from your heart. God will hear you, Jesus Christ will forgive your sins and enter your life. You will be a Christian.

"Dear God, I come to you as a person who recognizes my condition before you. I see that I am a sinner in need of a Savior. Jesus, I do believe that God raised You from the dead and I now invite you into my life. I confess Jesus as my Lord. I want to know You and be the Christian You have called me to be, according to Your definition. I thank You, in Jesus' Name. Amen."

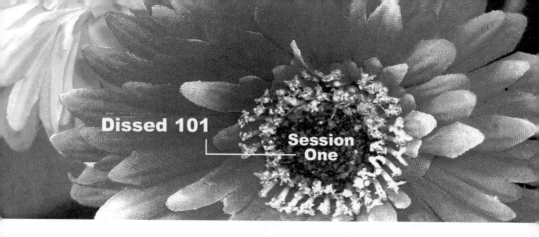

Dissed 101

Session One

When was the last time you got dissed? You know, dissed—being rejected, disrespected and dejected. If you are over the age of 35, you may not be familiar with the word. It's a fairly new word that the pop culture has embraced. Diss has many meanings; none are definitive. It's been used in rap, slang and urban language, and is simply an abbreviated form of some of the dis- words: disrespect, disparage, dismiss, disconnect, disregard. In our terms: rejected! Just like you, I know what it feels like to be dissed, rejected and overlooked.

How I Learned This Lesson

Loserville. I was a senior in high school and no one asked me to the prom! I was so bummed out! I was devastated and felt like a major reject! Ever had a lump in your throat for weeks at a time? Several months before the big night, all my friends were talking about their dresses and where they were going to dinner. They buzzed with excitement while I sat quietly, not even wanting to acknowledge that I wasn't going. Rejected. Humiliated. Embarrassed. Seriously dissed. That's how I felt.

I really hadn't dated anyone since ninth grade. So, why was I surprised? Somehow, I just hoped that someone would ask me to the senior prom. During that time, a spirit of rejection began to take hold in my life. I felt so unwanted. So ugly. So unlovable.

My parents had been divorced from the time I was in sixth grade; perhaps it was after my dad left that the seeds of rejection set in. (I was not aware of it and I doubt anyone

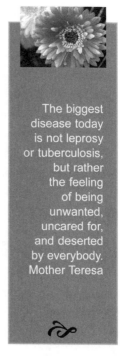

The biggest disease today is not leprosy or tuberculosis, but rather the feeling of being unwanted, uncared for, and deserted by everybody.
Mother Teresa

observing my life would have guessed how I felt.) On the outside, I was surrounded by a group of great girlfriends to hang with. Our group ran around with a group of boys and we all partied together most of our high school years. I was class president several times, played varsity basketball and enjoyed a fair degree of popularity in my school, but when it came to boyfriends—I felt like a reject. Not being asked to the prom took the cake. Now it was confirmed. I WAS a certified reject! Before you pull out your Kleenex to wipe the big salties . . . let me tell you the end of this pitiful story! About four weeks before prom, I was at my dad's during one of our weekend visits and he asked me about prom. I was very quiet and didn't say too much about it. He realized that I was devastated, so he did the most humiliating and the most wonderful thing!

Without my knowledge, he called one of his friends, who just happened to have an 18-year-old son, Kurt. My dad told Kurt about my dilemma and offered to pay him $100 if he would ask me to the prom. Is that mortifying or what? Is that the most pitiful thing you've ever heard? It's a good thing I didn't know about it, because this would have been my interpretation of the conversation: *"Hello, Kurt? This is Jerry. I have a huge favor to ask. My loser daughter is such a reject no one has asked her to the prom, and I beg you, I'll give you a hundred bucks if you will please take her to the stinkin' prom."* Well, Kurt was a nice guy (and I'm sure the $100 bucks didn't hurt either!), and he did ask me to the prom. I was thrilled to say yes! We went. Here's what I found out: the prom isn't THAT big of a deal. It was okay, but not the highlight of my life. I didn't find out about the "prom bribe" until about 5 years after the fact, and I was absolutely mortified and absolutely thrilled that my dad would do such a thing!

As it turned out in my life, God used this "prom" experience and other times I felt the pangs of rejection to take me on a wonderful journey with Him in His Word. I'd like to take you on a Bite Sized Bible Study adventure with me so that you, too, can enjoy a life free from any sense of rejection or inferiority!

Ever Been Dissed? Rejected? Overlooked?

Perhaps you've felt the same way. Dissed. Rejected. Overlooked. Maybe it wasn't the prom that confirmed your reject status; maybe it was something that created larger scars inside of you. Maybe you've been abused and mistreated by people you thought you could trust. Maybe you've been rejected by people because of your appearance, handicap, or your social or economic status. Perhaps you've felt rejected by a job promotion you didn't get, or maybe it was the broken engagement that broke your heart. Maybe you've been rejected by your parents. A lover? A boss? A professor? A friend? Rejected because you're too tall? Too short? Too skinny? Too fat? You don't fit the mold? Maybe complete strangers have rejected you! Rejected by people because of your faith in Jesus Christ?

If you're a parent, perhaps your children dissed you by talking back to you or making fun of your old-fashioned ways. If you're a student, maybe you get dissed at school just about every day when you wear the wrong clothes, hairstyle or shoes. In the adult world, at work or in the neighborhood you get dissed when people talk behind your back or don't invite you to the next party.

If you've ever been one of the last ones picked for a team; if you've ever asked someone out and heard the words "no"; if you've sat by the phone that never rang; if you've gotten a "Dear John/Dear Jane" letter; if anyone has ever hung up on you, not answered your e-mail, ignored you with the silent treatment; read you the riot act and welcomed you to Loserville; if you've ever received a "rejection" letter; been divorced, let go, fired, dumped, excluded or ostracized— you have felt rejected, dejected and dissed. Maybe it hasn't been anything dramatic, but perhaps a string of small things where you've just felt overlooked or unnoticed. Whatever it is, God wants to free you from a spirit of rejection.

Describe a time you felt rejected or dissed.

_____

_____

&**Nugget**& Just so you know, you're not alone. Everyone has felt rejected, even the most secure, confident, together person you know! Somewhere, sometime in their lives they have felt the pain of being rejected and not accepted. Experts tell us that 90% of the population walks around with a low self-esteem and self-image, and that tells us that there are lots and lots of people who feel rejected in some way.

Herbert Midgley wrote a song titled, "You Dissed Me," which describes the heartache of being rejected and putting our trust in the acceptance of others (used by permission of the author).

You dissed me. You dissed me.
You dissed me. Yes you did.

One time I loved you, One time I needed you,
One time I thought you were mine.

You dissed me. You dissed me. You dissed me. Yes you did.
Why did you leave me? Why did you hurt me?
Why did you walk out of my life?

You were so special to me. You were the one for me.
You were my life can't you see?

You dissed me. You dissed me.
You dissed me. Yes you did.

Maybe I'll learn. Maybe I'll see.
Maybe I'll be all alone.

You dissed me. You dissed me.
You dissed me. Yes you did.

Scrappergirl.com is a personal blog where this young person wrote a song titled, *Dissed*. It's all about the rejected rejecting others.

Don't wanna get your number

Not gonna give you mine

Don't want a conversation

Don't wanna waste my time

Don't wanna chill with you

Don't wanna be your friend

Don't think you're good looking

Quit trying to pretend

Quit asking me why

Unless you really wanna know

Don't care if this hurts

Let's get this show on the road

Your pants are out of style

You always wear that shirt

Quit itching right there

Attention! loser alert!!

Perhaps you've noticed that sometimes those who act the hardest on the outside feel the most rejected on the inside. Often people put up barriers to protect themselves from further rejection. They've learned that if they don't get close to people they can protect themselves from further heartbreak and pain. In effect, they attract the very thing they fear. As they install walls of bitterness, anger, criticism, sarcasm and toughness, they give off an air of self-sufficiency which pushes people further away and the rejection cycle continues.

The following attributes are characteristics of rejection or the fear of rejection, according to Drs. James and Constance Messina, (www.coping.org, used by permission of the authors).

1. *State of being of individuals who are over-dependent on the approval, recognition, or affirmation of others in order to feel good about themselves. In order to sustain personal feelings of adequacy these individuals are*

I am amazed by how many individuals mess up every new day with yesterday. They insist on bringing into today the failures of yesterday and in doing so pollute a potentially wonderful day.
Gary Chapman

constantly concerned with the reactions of others to them.

2. Irrational fear that others will not accept me for who I am, what I believe, and how I act.

3. Pervasive motivator for caution in my behavior and interactions with others.

4. State of mind that makes me incapable of doing or saying anything for fear of others' rejection, lack of acceptance, or disapproval.

5. Self-censoring attitude that inhibits creativity, productivity, and imagination in one's approach.

6. Driving force behind many people that keeps them from being authentic human beings. They are so driven by the need for acceptance of others that they lose their own identity in the process. They mimic the ways in which others act, dress, talk, think, believe, and function. They become the three-dimensional clones of the "role models" they so desperately need to emulate in order to gain acceptance.

7. Underlying process in the power of "peer pressure" that grabs hold and makes people act in stereotypic, "pop" culture, counter culture, punk, new wave, preppie, yuppie, and other styles. They crave recognition and acceptance from the reference group with whom they want to be identified.

8. Energy-robbing attitude that leads to self immobilization, self-defeating, and self-destructive behavior. This attitude encourages ongoing irrational thinking and behavior, resulting in personal stagnation, regression, and depression.

9. Driving force of some people for all actions in their lives. It plays a part in their choices concerning their education, career direction, work behavior, achievement level, interpersonal and marital relationships, family and community life, and the ways in which they spend leisure time.

10. Act of giving to others more power than I give to myself over how I feel about myself. What the others say or feel about me is the determinant of how I

feel about myself. I am completely at the mercy of others for how happy or sad I will be. My self-satisfaction and belief in myself is in their hands. Fear of rejection is the abdication of power and control over my own life.

Do any of these characteristics describe you? _____

In what ways do you see that you've had symptoms of rejection or the fear of rejection?

_____

Jesus knows exactly how we feel when we've been rejected. He was rejected. He was dissed by the religious leaders of the day. He understands, and yet He does not want us to be bound or controlled by rejection. Let's look at God's Word on this subject.

God Understands Rejection

1.   Isaiah 53:3-11

In this passage, underline any word or phrase that describes rejection, brokenness or hurt.

3 He was despised and rejected — a man of sorrows, acquainted with bitterest grief. We turned our backs on him and looked the other way when he went by. He was despised, and we did not care. 4 Yet it was our weaknesses he carried; it was our sorrows that weighed him down. And we thought his troubles were a punishment from God for his own sins! 5 But he was wounded and crushed for our sins. He was beaten that we might have peace. He was whipped, and we were healed! 6 All of us have strayed away like sheep. We have left God's paths to follow our own. Yet the LORD laid on him the guilt and sins of us all. 7 He was oppressed and treated harshly, yet he never said a word. He was led as a lamb to the slaughter. And as a sheep is silent before the shearers, he did not open his mouth. 8 From prison and trial they led him away to his death. But who among the people realized

*that he was dying for their sins — that he was suffering their
punishment? 9 He had done no wrong, and he never deceived anyone.
But he was buried like a criminal; he was put in a rich man's grave. 10
But it was the LORD's good plan to crush him and fill him with grief.
Yet when his life is made an offering for sin, he will have a multitude
of children, many heirs. He will enjoy a long life, and the LORD's plan
will prosper in his hands. 11 When he sees all that is accomplished by
his anguish, he will be satisfied. And because of what he has
experienced, my righteous servant will make it possible for many to be
counted righteous, for he will bear all their sins. NLT*

Jesus knows what it means to be rejected! He was despised and
rejected! He totally understands what it feels like to be hurt, excluded,
misunderstood, ignored and treated poorly. He was rejected by man,
and on the cross as He bore our sin, He was rejected by His Father. Do
you know why Jesus experienced rejection? He was rejected as our
substitute. He really didn't deserve to be rejected or despised, but He
took upon Himself all that would make a person unacceptable before
God so that we would not be rejected. He took what we really deserved!

It is the enemy's plan to create distance and separation between us and
God. He wants us to feel inferior and unacceptable to God. The last
thing the devil wants is for you to recognize and experience God's
acceptance, through Jesus Christ. This is the very reason Jesus came.
Because of sin, we were separated from God—we were rejected. Sin
would have kept us permanently separated from God, but Jesus took
our sin upon Himself and became our substitute. On the cross, He took
the punishment we deserved. Jesus was rejected so that we could be
accepted.

How did people treat Jesus according to verse 3? _____

Whose weaknesses and sorrows did He carry? _____

Why was He wounded and crushed? _____

Why was He beaten? _____

Why was He whipped? _____

Because of all that He experienced, what did He make possible? _____

_____

He made it possible for you and me to be accepted—to be found righteous and acceptable in God's sight and even among men.

Think about it. What would it mean to you if you were convinced that God accepted you?

_____

2.   Isaiah 61:1-3

Underline any phrase that describes healing, comfort and acceptance.

1 The Spirit of the Lord GOD is upon Me, Because the LORD has anointed Me To preach good tidings to the poor; He has sent Me to heal the brokenhearted, To proclaim liberty to the captives, And the opening of the prison to those who are bound; 2 To proclaim the acceptable year of the LORD, And the day of vengeance of our God; To comfort all who mourn, 3 To console those who mourn in Zion, To give them beauty for ashes, The oil of joy for mourning, The garment of praise for the spirit of heaviness; That they may be called trees of righteousness, The planting of the LORD, that He may be glorified. NKJV

Believe in dreams. Never believe in hurts... You can't let the grief and the hurts and the breaking experiences of life control your future decisions.
Robert H. Schuller

Jesus came to heal the brokenhearted! The rejected. The hurting. Aren't you glad? He came to bring liberty to those who have felt captive in areas of their lives. He came to free you from spiritual, emotional, physical and mental bondages and prison walls that have kept you locked up!

What type of "year" did Jesus come to proclaim? _____

⊱**Nugget**⊰ Notice that He came to preach the "acceptable" year! God wants you to know, by experience, the sense of acceptance and not rejection! God's acceptance means God's favor—God's favor means God's acceptance!

What do we receive as a result of this "acceptable" year?

_____

What does God want us to be called? _____

We'll look at the subject of "righteousness" in our next Session because this is such a huge subject as it relates to being free from the sense of rejection.

God Loves and Accepts You

1.   Isaiah 49:14-16

         Underline the words that describe God's love for you.

         14 Yet Jerusalem says, "The LORD has deserted us; the Lord has forgotten us." 15 "Never! Can a mother forget her nursing child? Can she feel no love for a child she has borne? But even if that were possible, I would not forget you! 16 See, I have written your name on my hand. NLT

         God promises that He won't desert, reject or forget you! He loves you like a mother loves her new baby!

Describe the love a new mother has for her nursing child. _____

_____

Why is it that He will not forget us? _____

What does it mean to you that He has written your name on His hand?

_____

2.   1 Chronicles 4:9-10

Underline the four things that Jabez prayed for.

9 And Jabez was more honourable than his brethren: and his mother called his name Jabez, saying, Because I bare him with sorrow. 10 And Jabez called on the God of Israel, saying, Oh that thou wouldest bless me indeed, and enlarge my coast, and that thine hand might be with me, and that thou wouldest keep me from evil, that it may not grieve me! And God granted him that which he requested. KJV

❧**Nugget**❧ Perhaps you've read the book *The Prayer of Jabez* and discovered this magnificent prayer! Jabez may have been acquainted with the sense of rejection or being dissed. Get this: his mother named him Jabez, which means "to grieve, sorrowful." Talk about feeling like an unwanted child! We don't know why his mother named him that. Perhaps she experienced great pain and sorrow giving birth and Jabez had to be reminded of that for the rest of his life. Perhaps she was a single mother who faced an unwanted pregnancy that caused her sorrow. We don't know what happened, but we know that Jabez started his life with a sense of grief and sorrow. The Amplified Bible refers to Jabez' name as: "sorrow maker." How would you like to be reminded of the pain, grief and sorrow your birth caused every time someone called your name? Can you imagine? Today it might be like being named, "Pain in the neck" or "Unwanted." That might make you feel just a little unacceptable and rejected! Maybe you can relate to Jabez. Perhaps your parents have told you that they didn't want you, or you've heard how much grief and pain you've caused others. Maybe you've been told that people wish you had never been born. It's painful to deal with those types of things, but God, through Jesus Christ, has provided healing and help for you.

Did you notice what Jabez did—in spite of his label? He prayed! He asked God to do something that a reject doesn't deserve!

What four things did Jabez ask God to do for him?

_____

_____

_____

_____

He asked God to bless him indeed. He asked God to enlarge his influence. He asked God to surround Him with His favor. He asked God to keep him from evil.

What did God do? _____

God granted his request! Do you think God loved Jabez more than He loves you?

How about you? Are you ready to get some help? Are you ready to call on God and begin the joy of being set free from any label or aroma of rejection? Make this your homework:

• Call on God.
• Ask God to bless you.
• Ask God to enlarge your influence for Him.

- Ask God to surround you with His hand of favor.
- Ask God to keep you wise and obedient in the place of protection from evil.

We've looked at Jabez and the sense of rejection he may have faced, let's talk about why we sometimes feel rejected. Why do we sometimes feel rejected or fear rejection? According to Drs. James and Constance Messina, of coping.org, those who feel rejection can be characterized by several factors, including:

1. Lack healthy self-concepts, self-worth, or self-esteem because they were never fully affirmed in their families of origin.

2. Have had a traumatic experience of rejection, for example, in a divorce or separation that deeply scarred them.

3. Have lacked appropriate role models in life who accepted them for who they really were.

4. Have never been exposed to healthy ways of dealing with conflict or disagreement.

5. Lack the social skills to adapt to a reference group.

6. Have suffered from social isolation in their early lives.

7. Lack certain personal accomplishments, which they feel set them apart and which contribute to their lack of self-confidence.

8. Have a physical condition that they believe makes them unattractive to others.

9. Have been told all their life that they were "second best" or different.

10. Fear that others will not accept them for who they are, what they believe or how they act. (Used by permission of the authors).

There are only two ways to live your life. One is as though nothing is a miracle. The other is as though everything is a miracle.
Albert Einstein

Obviously, there are different degrees to which people are affected by a sense of rejection. It can range from minor hurt feelings to major debilitating fear. The good news is that God promises that He will never reject you.

God Will Never Leave Or Reject You

1.   Ephesians 1:3-6

Underline the words, "chose" and "accepted in the Beloved."

3 Blessed be the God and Father of our Lord Jesus Christ, who has blessed us with every spiritual blessing in the heavenly places in Christ, 4 just as He chose us in Him before the foundation of the world, that we should be holy and without blame before Him in love, 5 having predestined us to adoption as sons by Jesus Christ to Himself, according to the good pleasure of His will, 6 to the praise of the glory of His grace, by which He made us accepted in the Beloved. NKJV

You need to ponder the phrase, "He chose us . . ." Can you grasp that? God picked you! He wants you! He doesn't reject you, but rather He chose you! Let that soak in; it's a nice thing to renew your mind to!

⊹Nugget⊹ I remember back in junior high we would go roller skating at the local rink where each night they would have the "Snowball Skate." This was the dreaded "somebody-please-pick-me" skate! All the girls would line up on the wall, and the boys would skate around and pick a girl to skate the Snowball Skate song with. I always hoped someone would pick me, but I usually ended up skating off the rink by myself—feeling like a reject—and then I'd stand on the sidelines watching all the girls who got picked skate with their dreamy boys! Well, guess what? God had a big "Snowball Skate" and He picked you! He saw you standing there, feeling inferior, insecure and lost, and He chose you!

What does this passage tell us we are "in the Beloved"? _____

23

We are accepted! Through our faith in Him, God has placed us in Christ and we are completely accepted by God! Let that soak in! When you get a grip on the reality that God has accepted you completely through your union with Christ, then it becomes less important to you if others accept or reject you!

ॐ**Nugget**ॐ God has not rejected you! He understands the reality of being rejected and brokenhearted – so much so that He took our place and identified with our sense of inferiority, unworthiness, rejection so that we could experience the reality of being chosen and accepted by God. He came to heal the brokenhearted and to let us know that the time of being "accepted" is at hand! You and I are accepted in Christ!

2.   John 6:37

Underline Jesus' promise to those who come to Him.

However, those the Father has given me will come to me, and I will never reject them. NLT

What will Jesus never do to you? _____

3.   Hebrews 13:5-6

Underline the word "never."

5 God has said, 'Never will I leave you; never will I forsake you.' 6 So we say with confidence, 'The Lord is my helper; I will not be afraid. What can man do to me?' NIV

What will God never do to you? _____

ॐ**Nugget**ॐ One of the ultimate forms of rejection is when someone you love leaves you. That is why divorce is so painful. To be rejected by someone you love is heartbreaking. As a baby Christian, I remember one night staying awake almost all night afraid that if I went to sleep God would leave me. Sometime during that night as I read my Bible, I stumbled on Hebrews 13:5, *"I will never leave you nor forsake you." NKJV* When I read that verse of Scripture, God filled me with peace and the assurance that He would never leave me. I've often thought that my fear of God leaving me was connected to my parents' divorce and my dad leaving our family; it was such a comfort to know that God will never leave us, even if someone we love does. Be encouraged if you've faced the heartbreak of divorce or the pain of watching someone you love walk out of your life. God will never walk out on you!

In this session, I trust you've begun to grasp the reality that God understands the pain and hurt of being dissed, rejected and overlooked, but through our union with Jesus Christ He's provided the very thing we need: Acceptance!

Scriptures To Chew On

Taking time to meditate on and memorize God's Word is invaluable. Hiding His Word in our hearts will strengthen us for the present and arm us for the future. Here are two verses to memorize and chew on this week. Write these verses on index cards and carry them with you this week. If you will post them in your bathroom, dashboard, desk, locker or other convenient places, you will find these Scriptures taking root in your heart.

"The Spirit of the LORD is upon Me, because He has anointed Me
to preach the gospel to the poor; He has sent Me to heal the brokenhearted,
to proclaim liberty to the captives and recovery of sight to the blind,
To set at liberty those who are oppressed;
to proclaim the acceptable year of the LORD."
Luke 4:18-19, NKJV

"Through the LORD's mercies we are not consumed,
because His compassions fail not.
They are new every morning; great is Your faithfulness."
Lamentations 3:22-23, NKJV

Group Discussion

1.   Describe a time in your life when your heart was broken by rejection or feeling overlooked. How did this experience affect you?

2.   Describe the way you would feel emotionally, mentally and spiritually if you knew and believed that God loved and accepted you unconditionally. What keeps you from believing this truth?

3.   Describe the importance of being accepted by God and how that spills over into your other relationships. In other words, what kind of pressure is put on relationships when people are not convinced that God loves and accepts them?

Personal Notes

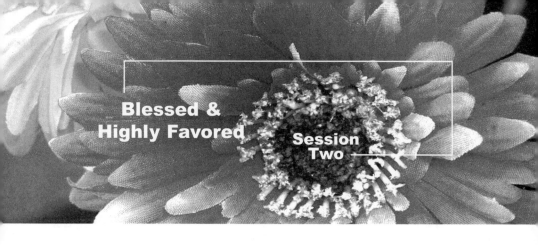

Who says you have to receive rejection? You can be the one who rejects rejection! What happens if you just choose to reject rejection? Author John Kandor wrote a great rejecting rejection letter, (www.jkador.com, used by permission of the author).

> *Dear ......,*
>
> *Thank you for your letter rejecting my application for employment with your firm.*
>
> *I have received rejections from an unusually large number of well qualified organizations. With such a varied and promising spectrum of rejections from which to select, it is impossible for me to consider them all. After careful deliberation, then, and because a number of firms have found me more unsuitable, I regret to inform you that I am unable to accept your rejection.*
>
> *Despite your company's outstanding qualifications and previous experience in rejecting applicants, I find that your rejection does not meet with my requirements at this time. As a result, I will be starting employment with your firm on the first of the month.*
>
> *Circumstances change and one can never know when new demands for rejection arise. Accordingly, I will keep your letter on file in case my requirements for rejection change.*

Never get in a spittin' match with a skunk. Even if you win, you come out smelling bad.
Unknown

Please do not regard this letter as a criticism of your qualifications in attempting to refuse me employment.

I wish you the best of luck in rejecting future candidates.

Sincerely, John Kador

Isn't that great? God wants us to reject rejection by realizing who we are in Him. When we are confident in who He has made us, we can give rejection the boot. We are accepted in Him. Not only does He accept us, He pursues us!

There is a great heartfelt song by Darlene Zschech titled, "Everything About You" that includes this interesting line about her husband, *". . . you chased me, I caught you."* I love that line! That's exactly what Jesus has done for us! He chased us and we caught Him! He chased us down with His desire to forgive our sins, declare us "righteous" and to surround us with His "favor." It's almost too good to be true; God first loved us and initiated a plan to "catch" us!

☙**Nugget**☙ I remember a time in my life when it occurred to me that Jesus chased me! He initiated. He chose me. He sought me. I was stunned! For some reason, I had thought that I was the one who sought Him and I was the one who accepted Him, but one day as I was singing and worshipping the Lord, He gave me this song I titled, "The Other Way Around" and reminded me that He <u>first</u> loved me!

The Other Way Around

I was the one, who thought that I found You,
but You were the One, and I was found by You.

I was the one, who thought that I sought Your face,
but You were the One, who sought me in the first place.

I was the one, who thought that I loved You,
but You were the One, that loved me first and true.

I was the one who thought I gave my life to You,
but You were the One, that gave Your life, My Redeemer, true.

All along, it was the other way around,
You sought me and chased me down.

You are the One, I now do see,
You loved me first and reached out to me.

I was the one, that You had in mind,
When You laid down Your life, on the cross divine.

You are the One that I worship and adore
And I am the one that longs for You more and more.

Let's look at how much God loves, favors and accepts us!

God Loves You

It sounds a bit cliché, doesn't it? Unfortunately, many people have not truly experienced God's love for themselves. Too many people see God as a big ogre or a mean judge ready to bop them when they mess up. The reality is that God loves you and has always loved you.

1.   Jeremiah 31:3

        Underline the phrases "I have loved you" and "I have drawn you."

        The LORD appeared to us in the past, saying: "I have loved you with
        an everlasting love; I have drawn you with loving-kindness." NIV

        How long has God loved you? _____

        What has He done with His loving-kindness? _____

        How has He done this in your life? _____

2.   Isaiah 62:2-5,12

Underline the phrases that describe your old name and the phrases that describe your new name.

2 . . . And the LORD will give you a new name. 3 The LORD will hold you in his hands for all to see — a splendid crown in the hands of God. 4 Never again will you be called the Godforsaken City or the Desolate Land. Your new name will be the City of God's Delight and the Bride of God, for the LORD delights in you and will claim you as his own. 5 Your children will care for you with joy, O Jerusalem, just as a young man cares for his bride. Then God will rejoice over you as a bridegroom rejoices over his bride. . . . 12 They will be called the Holy People and the People Redeemed by the LORD. And Jerusalem will be known as the Desirable Place and the City No Longer Forsaken. NLT

Perhaps, like Jabez (from our previous session), your name and identity was one of rejection and inferiority.

What did the Lord say He would do? _____

What would you not be called any longer? _____

What will you be called? _____

&**Nugget**& This is good news! This prophetic verse tells us about the future of the great city of Jerusalem, and it also tells us about our identity in Christ. Maybe it's time you began calling yourself what God calls you! In Jesus Christ, you are now called, "God's Delight, the Bride of God, Holy People, People Redeemed, Desirable, No Longer Forsaken." Think about it—God's delight! Desirable! Wow!

God Chose You

1.   John 15:16

        Underline the words "choose" and "chose."

        You did not choose Me, but I chose you and appointed you that you
        should go and bear fruit, and that your fruit should remain, that
        whatever you ask the Father in My name He may give you. NKJV

        Did we choose Jesus? _____

        Did Jesus choose us? _____

        What does it mean to be chosen? _____

        Why did He choose us? _____

2.   1 Corinthians 1:27-28

        Underline the word "chose."

        27 Isn't it obvious that God deliberately chose
        men and women that the culture overlooks and
        exploits and abuses, 28 chose these 'nobodies' to
        expose the hollow pretensions of the
        'somebodies'? The Message

        Who does God choose?

        _____

        What does this passage mean to you? _____

        _____

The
love
of God
is no mere
sentimental
feeling;
it is
redemptive
power!
Charles
Clayton
Morrison

3.   2 Thessalonians 2:13

Underline the words "God picked you."

Meanwhile, we've got our hands full continually thanking God for you, our good friends — so loved by God! God picked you out as his from the very start. Think of it: included in God's original plan of salvation by the bond of faith in the living truth. The Message

Why did God pick you?

_____

4.   1 Peter 2:9-10

Underline the word "chosen."

9 But you are the ones chosen by God, chosen for the high calling of priestly work, chosen to be a holy people, God's instruments to do his work and speak out for him, to tell others of the night-and-day difference he made for you — 10 from nothing to something, from rejected to accepted. The Message

Why did God choose you, according to this verse?

_____

God brought us from "nothing to something" and from

"_____ to _____"

What does that mean to you?

_____

_____

God Made You Righteous

1.   Romans 3:21-22

Underline the phrase "the righteousness of God."

21 But now the righteousness of God apart from the law is revealed, being witnessed by the Law and the Prophets, 22 even the righteousness of God, through faith in Jesus Christ, to all and on all who believe. NKJV

What does this passage call righteousness? _____

This passage says: righteousness is a revelation! This righteousness is given to us completely separate and apart from our ability to keep the Law, the Ten Commandments, the rules and regulations in the Bible!

Let's pray right now and ask God for the spirit of wisdom and revelation on this truth. *"Dear Father God, I ask You to give me the spirit of wisdom and revelation in obtaining the knowledge of righteousness. In Jesus' Name. Amen."*

Righteousness: Its basic definition means "the way in which man may attain a state approved of God."[1] It is also defined as, "the character or quality of being right or just"; it was formerly spelled "rightwiseness."[2]

☙**Nugget**☙ I like the way one preacher defined it: *to be righteous in Christ is to be able to stand before God without any sense of unworthiness, guilt or inferiority as though sin has never existed.* Are you convinced that God loves you? Because of His love for you and His acceptance of you in Jesus Christ, He has given you the great free gift of being righteous in His sight—of obtaining the "righteousness of God." Think about this! One of the greatest revelations you will ever receive from the Word of God is the reality of *righteousness.* Most people are sin-conscious; that is, they are primarily aware and conscious of their failings, their sins, their flaws and their mistakes which results in a sense of inferiority, unworthiness, condemnation and rejection. God does not want His children to be sin-conscious, but rather He wants us to be "righteousness-conscious." Too many Christians still see themselves as the "unworthy worm" they were before they accepted Jesus Christ and His forgiveness, and they have failed to see who they have become in Christ—brand new, forgiven and made righteous in His sight! The day you really understand "righteousness"—that God sees you in Christ as a person without any sense of inferiority as though you have never sinned—is a day of great freedom! That is a day of great joy! That is God's absolute will for you!

The "righteousness of God" is given to whom? _____

Is it for the select, perfect, super-Christians? _____

2.   2 Corinthians 5:21

Underline the phrase "the righteousness of God."

For He made Him who knew no sin to be sin for us, that we might become the righteousness of God in Him. NKJV

Jesus was made sin (and thus rejected and despised) for whom? _____

Why did He do this? _____

In Him, what have we become? _____

How righteous is God? _____

Describe a person who knows that he is righteous in God's sight:

_____

Can you believe this? Can you accept this reality? In God's sight, because you are in Christ, He sees you as righteous as He is! Can you feel the guilt, condemnation, inferiority and rejection sliding off you?

3. Romans 5:17

Underline the phrase "the gift of righteousness."

. . . how much more will those who receive God's abundant provision of grace and of the gift of righteousness reign in life through the one man, Jesus Christ. NIV

When we receive abundant grace and the gift of righteousness, what do we do in life?

❧**Nugget**❧ What's the bottom line? God loves you! He chased you. He loved you first! He initiated. When you receive His love by receiving Jesus Christ, He immediately sees you in Christ—accepted, righteous and surrounded with His favor!

God Favors You

Do you have a favorite memory? A favorite friend? A favorite place to vacation? A favorite Scripture? Has anyone ever done you a great favor? Perhaps it was something you didn't deserve or pay for, but for whatever reason someone decided to do you a favor that totally blessed your life.

You are God's favorite! All of His children are His favorites and He is constantly doing favors for us. We are favored by God, simply because we are in His Son, Jesus Christ. Jesus paid the price and we got a deal we didn't deserve.

❧**Nugget**❧ When God accepts us and gives us His righteousness, we are surrounded with His favor. God

What would you attempt to do if you knew you would not fail?
Dr. Robert Schuler

favors you! God's favor is a most wonderful thing—to have the God of the universe going to bat for you just because He loves you and has made you His righteousness is a great blessing! God's favor always has a purpose. When He favors you, it's because He has a divine, redemptive purpose in mind. Let's look at this.

1.   Psalm 5:12

In this passage, underline the word "favor."

For You, O LORD, will bless the righteous; with favor You will surround him as with a shield. NKJV

Are you righteous? _____

According to what we just studied, you are!

What do you base your righteousness on?

_____

What does God promise the righteous? _____

_____

How would you define "favor"? _____

_____

Favor: This word is large! It covers so much of God's goodness toward us. Favor means: "a pleasure, a delight, a favor, goodwill, acceptance, a will"[3].

When God surrounds you with favor, He surrounds you with acceptance! Consider that again: He surrounds you with favors! He surrounds you with pleasure and delight! God's favor gives you preferential treatment, open doors, opportunities, special benefits, promotions and goodness just because His favor surrounds you like a shield. Do you believe it? Isn't that an awesome reality?

2.   Proverbs 3:1-4

Underline the phrase "favor with both God and people."

1 My child, never forget the things I have taught you. Store my commands in your heart, 2 for they will give you a long and satisfying life. 3 Never let loyalty and kindness get away from you! Wear them like a necklace; write them deep within your heart. 4 Then you will find favor with both God and people, and you will gain a good reputation. NLT

Not only will God surround your life with His favor and acceptance, He will give you favor and acceptance in the eyes of people!

If we want favor with God and people, what does this passage tell us to focus on?

_____

_____

Who's Who

Here's a partial list of the Bible characters who received God's favor. Underline the name of each person/group that received favor and circle the type of favor they received if it is mentioned.

"But the LORD was with Joseph and showed him mercy, and He gave him favor in the sight of the keeper of the prison." Genesis 39:21, NKJV

"21 And I will give this people favor in the sight of the Egyptians; and it shall be, when you go, that you shall not go empty-handed. 22 But every woman

shall ask of her neighbor, namely, of her who dwells near her house, articles of silver, articles of gold, and clothing; and you shall put them on your sons and on your daughters. So you shall plunder the Egyptians. . . . 36 And the LORD had given the people favor in the sight of the Egyptians, so that they granted them what they requested. Thus they plundered the Egyptians." Exodus 3:21-22, 12:36, NKJV

"The king loved Esther more than all the other women, and she obtained grace and favor in his sight more than all the virgins; so he set the royal crown upon her head and made her queen instead of Vashti." Esther 2:17, NKJV

"Now God had brought Daniel into the favor and goodwill of the chief of the eunuchs." Daniel 1:9, NKJV

"Then the angel said to her, "Do not be afraid, Mary, for you have found favor with God." Luke 1:30, NKJV

What did God's favor do for these people of God? _____

Just like these believers did, hook up with God's favor! God will grant you favor, not because you deserve it, but simply because He loves and accepts you as His child. Expect God's favor in every area of your life!

Scriptures To Chew On

Taking time to meditate on and memorize God's Word is invaluable. Hiding His Word in our hearts will strengthen us for the present and arm us for the future. Here are two verses to memorize and chew on this week. Write these verses on index cards and carry them with you this week. If you will post them in your bathroom, dashboard, desk, locker or other convenient places, you will find these Scriptures taking root in your heart.

"For the LORD God is a sun and shield;
the LORD bestows favor and honor;
no good thing does he withhold from those whose walk is blameless."
Psalm 84:11, NIV

"For if by the one man's offense death reigned through the one, much more those who receive abundance of grace and of the gift of righteousness will reign in life through the One, Jesus Christ."
Romans 5:17, NKJV

Group Discussion

1.   Describe a time you "chased" someone you loved; or a time someone who loved you "chased" you. How would you describe the idea of being "chased"?

2.   Describe a time in your life when you lived under the weight of guilt, condemnation and a sense of inferiority or shame. In other words, how does it feel to be "sin-conscious" rather than "righteousness-conscious"? Have you discovered the freedom that comes from knowing you are completely righteous in Christ, as though sin has never existed?

3.   Describe a recent experience with God's "favor" in your life.

---

[1] From Thayer's Greek Lexicon, Electronic Database. Copyright © 2000, 2003 by Biblesoft, Inc. All rights reserved.

[2] From Vine's Expository Dictionary of Biblical Words, Copyright (c)1985, Thomas Nelson Publishers.

[3] From The Online Bible Thayer's Greek Lexicon and Brown Driver & Briggs Hebrew Lexicon, Copyright © 1993, Woodside Bible Fellowship, Ontario, Canada. Licensed from the Institute for Creation Research.

Personal Notes

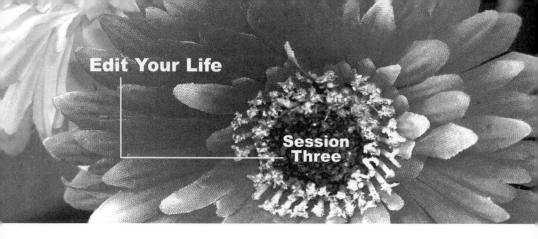

Edit Your Life

Session Three

I hope by now you are convinced that God loves and accepts you! Now the question is, how does this become practical and tangible in your life? How does this become more than just the greatest sounding theory you have ever heard? I've got good news for you. If you've struggled with feelings of rejection, you can be transformed. You can be a different person. You can feel different. You can think differently. You can literally be changed into another person!

I know this from experience! I am a different person today. I have experienced God's transforming power in my life. As I said, although on the outside no one would know it, internally I really struggled with a sense of rejection in my early Christian life, until I began to get a hold of the truths in this study. God's Word transformed me and I have walked in the reality of God's acceptance and an awareness of His goodness ever since.

If you've felt the heaviness of rejection or paralyzing hopelessness, that can change for you! If you've felt unlovable and overlooked you can experience the reality of feeling loveable. None of us want to feel the pain of rejection. By now, perhaps you are beginning to experience the reality of being accepted by God. That's a good thing!

Are you ready to edit your life? Reinvent yourself? Are you willing to cooperate with God and watch His Word transform your life in this area?

> When you're through changing, you're through.
> Bruce Barton

You Can Be Transformed

1.   Romans 12:2

In this passage, underline the phrase "be transformed."

And do not be conformed to this world, but be transformed by the renewing of your mind, that you may prove what is that good and acceptable and perfect will of God. NKJV

How would you describe being "transformed"? _____

_____

Transformed: The Greek word for this is: "metamorphoo." It means to transform (literally or figuratively, "metamorphose"). It's also translated as change, transfigure, transform.[1]

❧**Nugget**❧ How transformed can you be? In various areas of your life, you can be as transformed as a caterpillar that turns into a butterfly! Did you study caterpillars and butterflies in grade school? You know the process of metamorphosis, right? A caterpillar spins a cocoon and the chrysalis is formed to facilitate the transformation of this caterpillar into a butterfly! This transformation is amazing. Now, let me ask you a question: have you ever confused a caterpillar with a butterfly? Of course not. Why? Because the process of transformation was so dramatic that the butterfly does not look anything like a caterpillar! The same thing is true when God's transforming power, His supernatural metamorphosis, goes to work in your life. You will be changed to such a degree that the new "accepted you" will not look anything at all like the old "rejected you"!

According to this passage, how are we transformed? _____

_____

How would you define "renewing of the mind"? _____

_____

Renewing of your mind: Literally this means the "renovation" of your mind![2]

God wants you to renovate your mind to His Word! He wants you to do a major "fixer upper" job on your thinking by replacing the old, negative, rejected thoughts with the new, true, accepted thoughts His Word is loaded with!

Have you ever been involved in a home renovation project? Describe it.

_____

It takes work to renovate!

Are you ready to cooperate with God and His Word and put forth the effort it takes to renew or renovate your mind?

_____

☙**Nugget**❧ You need to get this! The primary way you experience transformation in any area of your life is by renovating, reprogramming and renewing your mind with God's Word! It's that simple and it's that powerful. As you begin to install new thoughts from God's Word into your mind regarding your acceptance in Christ, you will see the old "caterpillar you" transformed into a new "butterfly you"! For example, when you read Ephesians 1, which tells you that you are "accepted in the beloved", you need to begin to renovate your mind with that very thought. To do this you begin meditating on the reality that because you are a Christian in Christ, God accepts you completely. As you take time to ponder this thought, imagine what being accepted by God would look like, smell like and feel like; as you "paint" your mind with this Word from God, you will find yourself being transformed from the inside out.

This new thought of acceptance will eventually demolish the old thought of rejection, your mind will be renovated and you will be transformed. The "rejected caterpillar" will be transformed into an "accepted butterfly."

2.   1 Samuel 10:6-11

Underline the phrase "you will be changed into a different person."

6 The Spirit of the LORD will come upon you in power, and you will prophesy with them; and you will be changed into a different person. 7 Once these signs are fulfilled, do whatever your hand finds to do, for God is with you. 8 'Go down ahead of me to Gilgal. I will surely come down to you to sacrifice burnt offerings and fellowship offerings, but you must wait seven days until I come to you and tell you what you are to do.' 9 As Saul turned to leave Samuel, God changed Saul's heart, and all these signs were fulfilled that day. 10 When they arrived at Gibeah, a procession of prophets met him; the Spirit of God came upon him in power, and he joined in their prophesying. 11 When all those who had formerly known him saw him prophesying with the prophets, they asked each other, 'What is this that has happened to the son of Kish? Is Saul also among the prophets?' NIV

What happened to Saul? _____

What was it that changed Saul? _____

What did Saul's old friends say? _____

What do you think was different about Saul? _____

☙**Nugget**☙ We see the power of God changing Saul into a different person! Notice it was God's Spirit coming upon Saul that changed him. We might say it this way today: when you allow God's Presence through His Spirit and His Word to saturate your life, you will be changed! When the people that formerly knew Saul saw him, they couldn't believe it!

They wanted to know what had happened! This can be true of you, too! God will change you to such a degree that your old friends will scratch their heads and try to figure you out!

3.   2 Corinthians 3:18

Underline the word "transfigured."

And all of us, as with unveiled face, [because we] continued to behold [in the Word of God] as in a mirror the glory of the Lord, are constantly being transfigured into His very own image in ever increasing splendor and from one degree of glory to another; [for this comes] from the Lord [Who is] the Spirit. AMP

If we continue to spend time renovating our minds to God's Word, the mirror, what will happen to us?

_____

What will we be transfigured or transformed into?

_____

The good news is that you don't have to stay the way you are! You don't have to feel or be rejected! God has shown us how to be transformed! We can experience a supernatural metamorphosis through the power of God's Word! Let the renovation project begin.

Opportunity is missed by most people because it is dressed in overalls and looks like work. Thomas Edison

You can be transformed and you don't have to take rejection lying down! As you begin to see your value in God's eyes you will be transformed into the confident person He sees you to be in Him.

↦**Nugget**↤   There is no doubt that God's Word and His power can change your life. At the same time, we also want to be honest with ourselves and God. If we are feeling rejected or overlooked or dissed, is there a reason? Are we doing anything that would cause others to reject or diss us? Are we being an irritant? Self-absorbed? Critical? A stick in the mud? Boring? A drag? A big pain in the drain? Face it; no one wants to be around a "downer" or the person having a constant pity party. Are you making yourself enjoyable to be around? A pleasure to work with? Easy to talk to? We have a responsibility to be the type of person that exhibits godly qualities people would enjoy being around.

Whatever the reason, history or cause of our feeling rejected or dissed, through the power of God's Word we can edit our lives. We can reinvent ourselves. We can "do over." It will require us to agree with God. We will have to think differently which will take some effort on our part, but the results will be a dramatic transformation!

Scriptures To Chew On

Taking time to meditate on and memorize God's Word is invaluable. Hiding His Word in our hearts will strengthen us for the present and arm us for the future. Here are two verses to memorize and chew on this week. Write these verses on index cards and carry them with you this week. If you will post them in your bathroom, dashboard, desk, locker or other convenient places, you will find these Scriptures taking root in your heart.

"Now you're dressed in a new wardrobe.
Every item of your new way of life is
custom-made by the Creator, with his label on it.
All the old fashions are now obsolete."
Colossians 3:10, The Message

"So if the Son sets you free, you will be free indeed."
John 8:36, NIV

Group Discussion

1. Describe a home renovation project you have experienced; the blood, sweat and tears! How is this compared to the idea of renovating our minds?

2. Describe the changes others have seen in your life since Jesus became the Lord of your life. When your old friends saw you, what changes did they notice?

3. Describe the change and transformation that would be evident in a person that went from feeling rejected and overlooked to being accepted and confident. How would you describe their disposition, communication and general self-esteem?

---

[1] Biblesoft's New Exhaustive Strong's Numbers and Concordance with Expanded Greek-Hebrew Dictionary. Copyright © 1994, 2003 Biblesoft, Inc. and International Bible Translators, Inc.

[2] as above

Personal Notes

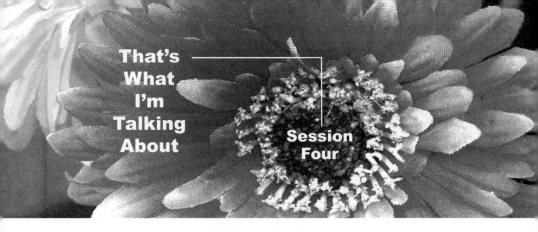

That's
What
I'm
Talking
About

Session
Four

When I was in my mid-twenties and single, I had a desire to meet my Mr. Wonderful, be married and start a family, but the thoughts and feelings of rejection that went through my mind were sometimes paralyzing and the enemy used this to discourage me. At this time I learned a life-changing truth.

As I meditated on God's Word regarding His acceptance and favor, I started to see myself the way God does, as accepted, loveable and desirable. But I realized that it was not enough to just believe what the Word said about me; I needed to **say** what the Word said about me. Getting a grip on my lip was a huge turning point in my Christian life!

Like many sincere Christian girls, I had been praying for many years about the man I would marry. At the same time, I was growing in my walk with the Lord, Christian character and maturity. Yet, in my case, because the thoughts of rejection had been such a stronghold in my life—I had gotten into a bad habit of thinking, saying and feeling like no one would want me, which really caused me to struggle in my belief that anyone would! I knew I needed to renew my mind with God's thoughts and get my mouth speaking words that would turn the boat around. I realized I needed to take drastic measures to complete the process of supernatural transformation in this area of my life!

One day, I decided on a phrase that would become my new slogan! To some, this might sound ridiculous or even arrogant, but for me it was a life raft and it kept me afloat to the shores of acceptance and meeting Mr. Wonderful!

Cold words freeze people, and hot words scorch them, and bitter words make them bitter, and wrathful words make them wrathful. Kind words also produce their image on men's souls; and a beautiful image it is. They smooth, and quiet, and comfort the hearer.
Blaise Pascal

My new phrase? *"They all want me—bad!"* Since inside myself I felt like, *"No one will ever want me,"* I knew that I needed to change that thought with a new statement. So, it started as a tongue-in-cheek joke at first, when I said, *"They all want me—bad!"* At that time, I didn't feel like anyone wanted me at all, but I knew I had to get my mouth in agreement with my desires and faith. Of course, the enemy was right there with his negative thoughts, *"Yeah right . . . they all want you . . . sure they do . . . who are you kidding? No one wants you, remember?"* I just ignored those thoughts and continued to say to myself and my closest friends, *"They all want me—bad!"* It was a faith confession! As I continued to say this phrase, the most amazing thing happened: my thinking started to change and I started to feel that maybe someday someone would want me after all. I continued to say, *"They all want me—bad!"* The more I said it, the more I started to believe it. And get this: the more I said it, the more I actually began to expect it!

Guess what? Within a short time, I met Jeff, my Mr. Wonderful who became my husband, and you'll never believe what he told me a few months after we were engaged! In one of our intimate moments, he said, verbatim, *"I want you bad!"* Can you believe that? I can! God has given me "exceedingly more than I could ask or think" in Jeff. He is such a picture of God's love and acceptance in my life; it's almost unbelievable! But what makes it believable is that God promises us that we can be changed by the renewing of our minds, and as we'll see in this study our words play a starring role in that transformation.

Your Words Are Shaping Your World

1.   Proverbs 6:2

        Underline the phrase "snared by the words of your mouth."

        You are snared by the words of your mouth; you are taken by the words of your mouth. NKJV

        What can the words of our mouth do to us? _____

Unfortunately, we are often being snared by our own words. When we say things like, *"I am so ugly." "That just kills me." "He's driving me crazy" "I'm such a klutz." "No one will ever ask me out"* and the like, we are ensnaring ourselves with our words.

What negative words, that are contrary to God's Word, are you saying about yourself and your life?

_____

Are you willing to stop saying those negative words? _____

2.   Hebrews 11:3

Underline the phrase that tells us what framed the world.

By faith we understand that the worlds were framed by the word of God, so that the things which are seen were not made of things which are visible. NKJV

What framed the world? _____

What were the visible things made with? _____

☙**Nugget**☙ Let's get the picture. God made the visible world with things that are not visible! He created the seen from the unseen. How did He do this? He framed (sounds like a renovation word, doesn't it?) the world with His words! He spoke words like, *"Let there be light . . ."* and there was light! He spoke words like, *"Let us make man in our image . . ."* and He made man! God's spoken word created the reality of the world in which we now live! God's Word framed the world!

This principle of speaking God's Word is still in effect! God's Word still has the power to frame our worlds! God created us in His image and likeness and our words have the power to frame our world.

What type of world have you been framing (for yourself and others) with God's words?

_____

As we speak God's Word in our own lives we will find that our "world" will become more congruent with God's Word and God's will. Let's look at the power of words that God has given to us.

3.   Proverbs 18:21

Underline the phrase "the tongue has the power."

The tongue has the power of life and death, and those who love it will eat its fruit. NIV

Does our tongue have power? _____

Our tongue has what kind of power? _____

What fruit will we eat in our lives? _____

Can you see that your words will create life or death in your world? We eat the fruit of our words. If you don't like the fruit of your life, reflect for a moment and think about the words you have been saying.

When I was constantly saying things like, *"I feel so rejected, no one ever asks me out,"* guess what my fruit was? No one ever asked me out! When I changed what my tongue was saying, my world began to change!

4.   James 3:3-6

Underline the words "bit," "rudder" and "spark."

3 When we put bits into the mouths of horses to make them obey us, we can turn the whole animal. 4 Or take ships as an example. Although they are so large and are driven by strong winds, they are steered by a very small rudder wherever the pilot wants to go. 5 Likewise the tongue is a small part of the body, but it makes great boasts. Consider what a great forest is set on fire by a small spark. 6 The tongue also is a fire, a world of evil among the parts of the body. It corrupts the whole person, sets the whole course of his life on fire, and is itself set on fire by hell. NIV

This passage is talking about the power of the tongue in a negative way—it can corrupt the whole person! On the other hand, we see the power of the tongue to direct our lives.

What does the bit do in the horse's mouth? _____

_____

Who determines what the bit does? _____

What does the rudder do on the ship?

_____

Who determines what the rudder does?

_____

What does a spark do?

_____

Who determines the start of a spark?

_____

Life is the sum of all your choices. Albert Camus

Like the bit in the horse's mouth and like the rudder on a ship, or a spark—our tongue can direct the course of a life, as well!

What direction is your tongue taking you? What port are your words taking you to? What fires are you starting with your mouth? Give some thought to the power of your words and make a decision to say the things about your life that agree with God's Word!

Speak To Your Mountain

1.   Mark 11:22-23

Underline the words "says," "say," "whosoever" and "whatever."

22 So Jesus answered and said to them, 'Have faith in God. 23 For assuredly, I say to you, whoever says to this mountain, "Be removed and be cast into the sea," and does not doubt in his heart, but believes that those things he says will be done, he will have whatever he says.'
NKJV

❧**Nugget**❧ Jesus revealed the power of our words in this passage! If you read Mark 11:13-24, you will see that the context of Jesus' lesson was the power of His speaking words to a fig tree! Jesus saw a fig tree that didn't have any fruit and He spoke words to that fig tree—telling it that it would not produce fruit again. He spoke loud enough for His disciples to hear! The next day when the disciples saw the fig tree that Jesus had cursed withered up from its roots, they were amazed that the tree had obeyed His Words! Jesus responded to the disciples by saying, "Have faith in God!" In verses 23 and 24, Jesus then defines what faith in God looks like! A person with faith in God would speak to mountains! This person would believe the things he said. This person would have the things he said! Jesus made it so simple that unfortunately, Christians have stumbled over this idea of speaking words of faith by explaining it away and deleting it from their thinking and their theology!

According to this passage, is Jesus the only one who has the power or authority to speak words to things?

_____

Who did Jesus authorize with the power to speak to mountains? _____

According to verse 23, what can "whosoever" have? _____

_____

Did Jesus say "speak to God about your mountain" or "speak to the mountain directly"?

_____

❧**Nugget**❧ Many times people speak to God about their mountain, but Jesus told us to speak to the mountain by our faith in God!

Where are you not supposed to doubt? _____

When you speak words, what are you supposed to believe?

_____

If you believe what you say, what will you have?

_____

Ok, so what does this mean to us? It reminds us that our words have power to change our lives and circumstances! If you're facing mountains, you've got an answer! If the mountain of rejection is staring you in the face, get busy talking to that mountain! Start quoting God's Word over your life! Make your mouth and heart agree with God! He says you're accepted, so you better start saying, "I am accepted!"

2.   Psalm 107:2

Underlined the phrase "say so."

Let the redeemed of the LORD say so . . . NKJV

What are the redeemed supposed to do? _____

Have you been redeemed from rejection to acceptance? _____

Have you made it your practice to "say so"? _____

⮞**Nugget**⮜ Your words have power whether you like it or not! Where you are in life today is a direct result of the words you spoke yesterday. Perhaps you will want to give some serious thought to changing your words and reframing your world with God's Word! Perhaps it's time to start talking to your mountain. Maybe it's time to be a better captain of the ship of your life. Get your mouth in agreement with God and His Word.

Scriptures To Chew On

Taking time to meditate on and memorize God's Word is invaluable. Hiding His Word in our hearts will strengthen us for the present and arm us for the future. Here are two verses to memorize and chew on this week. Write these verses on index cards and carry them with you this week. If you will post them in your bathroom, dashboard, desk, locker or other convenient places, you will find these Scriptures taking root in your heart.

"You are snared by the words of your mouth;
You are taken by the words of your mouth."
Proverbs 6:2, NKJV

"A man will be satisfied with good by the fruit of his mouth..."
Proverbs 12:14, NKJV

Group Discussion

1.   What self-defeating words and phrases have kept you in bondage to feelings of rejection?

2.   If you had to write a 60-second commercial for the "new" you, what would you say about your life? Write a commercial telling others why they should want you in their lives.

3.   If you had to write a 60-second commercial for one of the people in your small group, what would you say about them? Write a commercial telling others why they would want this person in their lives.

Personal Notes

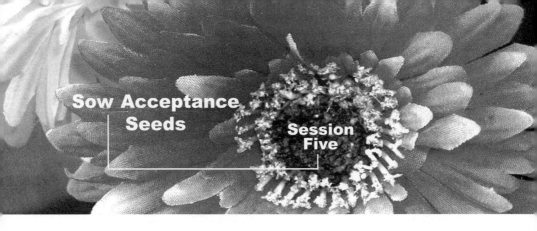

Sow Acceptance Seeds

Session Five

I love spring! After a cold Michigan winter it's great to see the daffodils and tulips spring up. I am constantly amazed at the miracle of how planting a bulb in the fall can result in a tulip in the spring. God's law of sowing and reaping, seedtime and harvest is one of His best gifts to mankind! We do reap what we sow and it's no less true in this area of acceptance.

One of the best ways to overcome your own weakness in this area is by simply sowing acceptance into the lives of others. Are you ready to "plant" seeds of love and acceptance? Let's turn the tables a bit and think about those around us. How can we help others experience acceptance? God created us to have relationships with others. Rich, intimate interpersonal relationships are one of God's most wonderful gifts. To reap these kinds of relationships, we must sow. How can we sow acceptance into the lives of others? It's easier than you think.

Sow Interest

As Dale Carnegie once said, *"You can make more friends in two months by becoming interested in other people than you can in two years of trying to get other people interested in you."*[1] I believe this is the most misunderstood secret to mutually enjoyable personal relationships. Think about it. When was the last time someone took note of the affairs, challenges, projects, dreams, events and dynamics of your world and asked you a meaningful question about your life? And . . . then continued to show their interest by asking several good follow-up questions? If so, you have a friend who is interested in your life.

You find yourself refreshed by the presence of cheerful people. Why not make an honest effort to confer that pleasure on others?
Lydia M. Child

I would bet that for most of you this type of conversation has not taken place in a long time. In fact, it is likely that the most recent conversations you have had with family, friends or co-workers have revolved around them telling you stories about them. If you are a good friend, you asked them questions showing your interest in their lives. My guess is that very few of you can honestly think of a person in your life that is consistent in asking you anything more than surface, cursory or courtesy questions. Why? Being interested in others and sowing acceptance in others goes against our selfish nature.

≈**Nugget**≈   Most people want to feel noticed, liked, accepted, appreciated and approved of by the people important to them. We want people to want us. We have a need to know and be known. People want to disclose themselves to someone who is interested. All the human behavior and psychology experts will tell you that self-disclosure is a basic need of human beings. This creates a feeling of closeness between people.

If we sow interest in others in an atmosphere of love and acceptance, we'll find a whole new level of rich relationships opens up to us and this replaces the fear of rejection.

I like what Christian author and founder of the Family Dynamics Institute, Joe Beam said in his article "Becoming Vulnerable", (www.familydynamics.net, used by permission of the author):

"Removing all masks to let another see who we really are ('warts and all') means risking everything in that relationship. If the other person doesn't accept us when they encounter our undisguised selves, we feel absolute rejection. We likely won't continue the relationship, even if the other person wants to, because we know that he or she has seen the true us and been repulsed by the discovery. So how do we grow past that fear and decide to reveal our true selves? We do it in stages. We start by sharing facts that are non-threatening; facts that we feel won't be reacted to negatively. As we share those innocuous facts of our lives (e.g. "I was born in the USA,") we register every reaction of the person to whom we share. Any lack of interest or hint of displeasure on their part causes us to stop the process. We're certainly not going to reveal potentially threatening facts (e.g. "When I was a kid I was arrested,") if we note any

disinterest or rejection as we share innocuous facts. On the other hand, as we register interest and acceptance we tend to reveal more threatening facts. We can become so trusting of the seemingly unconditional acceptance of the other person that we tell him or her things about ourselves we've never told anyone."

When we sow interest in others, we help them to blossom in healthy ways, and we are bound to eventually reap the same. What does God's Word tell us about helping others overcome the hurt of rejection, dejection and being dissed by sowing acceptance and interest into their lives?

The Apostle Paul was good at sharing his heart and being vulnerable with others. Listen to how he communicated the Gospel of Jesus Christ and his love, acceptance and care.

Cultivate Vulnerability In Yourself and Others

How vulnerable and transparent are you? Perhaps we need to ask ourselves some honest questions. For example, do you tend to open up to and confide in the people in your life, or do you keep tight-lipped? We all realize that there is a need for balance and learning how to navigate the tension between spilling our deepest feelings to total strangers and keeping an unhealthy distance from our friends and family. Self-disclosure, vulnerability and transparency is necessary for healthy relationships.

1.   2 Corinthians 6:11-13

Underline the phrases "spoken freely," "opened wide our hearts" and "not withholding our affection."

11 We have spoken freely to you, Corinthians, and opened wide our hearts to you. 12 We are not withholding our affection from you, but you are withholding yours from us. 13 As a fair exchange—I speak as to my children—open wide your hearts also. NIV

I love how the Living Bible translates this passage: *11 Oh, my dear Corinthian friends! I have told you all my feelings; I love you with all my heart. 12 Any coldness still between us is not because of any lack of love on my part but because your love is too small and does not reach out to me and draw me in. 13 I am talking to you now as if you truly were my very own children. Open your hearts to us! Return our love! TLB*

What three things did Paul do to cultivate vulnerability?

_____

_____

_____

Do you "speak freely" with others? _____

Do you "open wide your heart" to others? _____

Do you "withhold your affection" from others? _____

In what ways can you be more vulnerable in your relationships?_____

_____

2.   1 Thessalonians 2:8

Underline the phrase "share with you."

We loved you so much that we were delighted to share with you not only the gospel of God but our lives as well, because you had become so dear to us. NIV

What two things should we share with others? _____

_____

In your relationships, how do you share the Gospel and your own life?

_____

_____

How did Paul describe his feelings for these believers?

How To Be Genuinely Interested In Others

1.   Philippians 2:19-22

Underline the phrase "genuinely interested in your welfare and devoted to your interests."

19 But I hope and trust in the Lord Jesus soon to send Timothy to you, so that I may also be encouraged and cheered by learning news of you. 20 For I have no one like him [no one of so kindred a spirit] who will be so genuinely interested in your welfare and devoted to your interests. 21 For the others all seek [to advance] their own interests, not those of Jesus Christ (the Messiah). 22 But Timothy's tested worth you know, how as a son with his father he has toiled with me zealously in [serving and helping to advance] the good news (the Gospel). AMP

The Living Bible says it this way:

20 There is no one like Timothy for having a real interest in you; 21 everyone else seems to be worrying about his own plans and not those of Jesus Christ.

According to verse 20, what made Timothy stand out?

_____

_____

There are two kinds of people in the world— those who walk into a room and say, 'There you are'— and those who say, 'Here I am!' Abigail Van Buren

Are people like Timothy hard to find or commonplace?

_____

What was Timothy truly interested in? _____

_____

Was his interest "canned," "fake" or "shallow"? _____

What were others interested in? _____

In what ways could you be more like Timothy to the people in your life?

_____

_____

2.   Philippians 2:4

Underline the phrase "be interested in others."

Don't just think about your own affairs, but be interested in others, too, and in what they are doing. TLB

What does this tell us concerning our interest in our own lives? _____

_____

What part of others' lives are we to be interested in? _____

3.   John 16:5-6

Underline the phrase "none of you seems interested."

5 But now I am going away to the one who sent me; and none of you seems interested in the purpose of my going; none wonders why. 6 Instead you are only filled with sorrow. TLB

What were the disciples not interested in? _____

What consumed their interest? _____

In what ways are we often consumed with our own issues, sorrows, "pity parties" and not aware of the interests of those around us?

_____

4.   Zechariah 7:6

Underline the phrase "I'm interested in people."

And when you held feasts, was that for me? Hardly. You're interested in religion, I'm interested in people. The Message

What's the bottom line on what God is interested in? _____

⪻**Nugget**⪼   When you and I show an interest in others, we are acting like God. We stand out because, as the Apostle Paul said, there are not many people like Timothy who will naturally care for the interests of others. Let's be the kind of people that overcome our own sense of rejection by sowing acceptance and interest into the lives of others. As a result, we will reap our own harvest of acceptance, too!

If You Want To Have Friends, Be Friendly

1.   Proverbs 18:24

Underline the phrase "be friendly."

A man who has friends must himself be friendly, but there is a friend who sticks closer than a brother. NKJV

If you want to have friends, what must you be? _____

How can you sow "friendliness" into the people in your life? _____

_____

2.   John 15:11-13

Underline the phrase that describes what friends do for each other.

11 I have told you this so that my joy may be in you and that your joy may be complete. 12 My command is this: Love each other as I have loved you. 13 Greater love has no one than this, that he lay down his life for his friends. NIV

What does Jesus want to give us? _____

If we want to be filled with joy, how are we to love others? _____

How can we love our friends? _____

In what ways will you start sowing acceptance in their lives?

_____

Scriptures To Chew On

Taking time to meditate on and memorize God's Word is invaluable. Hiding His Word in our hearts will strengthen us for the present and arm us for the future. Here are two verses to memorize and chew on this week. Write these verses on index cards and carry them with you this week. If you will post them in your bathroom, dashboard, desk, locker or other convenient places, you will find these Scriptures taking root in your heart.

*"So this is my prayer: that your love will flourish and that you will
not only love much but well. Learn to love appropriately.
You need to use your head and test your feelings
so that your love is sincere and intelligent, not sentimental gush.
Live a lover's life, circumspect and exemplary,
a life Jesus will be proud of: bountiful in fruits from the soul,
making Jesus Christ attractive to all,
getting everyone involved in the glory and praise of God."
Philippians 1:9-11, The Message*

*"And may the Master pour on the love
so it fills your lives and splashes over on everyone around you,
just as it does from us to you."
1 Thessalonians 3:12, The Message*

Group Discussion

1. Describe a time that someone sowed friendship and acceptance into your life.

2. Describe the challenges and strategies of sowing acceptance with others in these settings:

    - at a party   - at school functions   - at work
    - at church   - in Bible studies   - at reunions
    - in neighborhood   - with strangers   - with family

3. Describe, in general, a time you were vulnerable with a friend and how it knit your friendship.

---

[1] Carnegie, Dale. How to Win Friends and Influence People. New York: Pocket Books, 1990.

68

Personal Notes

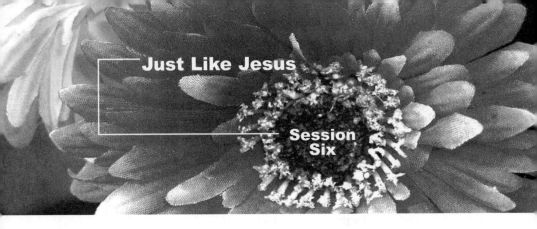

Some rejection is inevitable! Jesus told us that. It's true that because of our union with Jesus Christ we are totally accepted by God. At the same time, because of our alliance with Jesus Christ, we will experience rejection by others. People will mock and insult and distance themselves from us because of our faith in Jesus Christ. Because of our identification with Him, we will face persecution and rejection. When this happens, Jesus told us to be happy about it! It's a confirmation that you're a Christian!

Have you ever experienced this? Have you had people look down their noses at you because of your faith in Jesus Christ? I have. Just like you, I've lost friends. I've been ostracized. Looked down on. Ignored. Laughed at. Talked about. Made fun of. Dissed. Rejected. Overlooked.

If you are living the Christian life and carrying a solid Christian testimony you are going to face persecution and rejection. We are told "all who live godly in Christ will suffer persecution." So, you can expect this type of rejection if you live a godly life. This is the "good" kind of rejection.

If you're going through hell, keep going. Winston Churchill

☙**Nugget**☙ Here's a thought to consider: be sure, if you are "persecuted," that it is because of your good Christian testimony and not your flaky, obnoxious, self-righteous behavior! We all know Christians who have done more harm than good to the cause by their bizarre Christian behavior. At the same time, just be aware that no matter how good your intentions and how gracious your approach, sometimes you will be misunderstood, and people may reject you because they perceive you as flaky, obnoxious and self-righteous. Just be sure they don't have any evidence to support their case! Be a bold, loving, gracious Christian and be prepared for some flack!

In some places around the world people are experiencing severe persecution for their faith in Jesus Christ, to the point of torture and death. In other places, the persecution is mild in comparison. In either case, Jesus had a lot to say about believers being rejected by the world. Let's look at it.

If They Rejected Jesus, Guess What?

1.   Matthew 5:10-12

In this passage, underline the words "persecuted," "insult," "persecute" and "falsely say."

10 Blessed are those who are persecuted because of righteousness, for theirs is the kingdom of heaven. 11 Blessed are you when people insult you, persecute you and falsely say all kinds of evil against you because of me. 12 Rejoice and be glad, because great is your reward in heaven, for in the same way they persecuted the prophets who were before you. NIV

How would you describe persecution? _____

_____

There is a definite sense of feeling rejected when people insult you because of your faith in Jesus Christ.

What are we supposed to do when we are rejected because of our faith?

_____

What are we promised? _____

2.   John 17:14-19

Underline the phrase "the world has hated them."

14 I have given them your word and the world has hated them, for they are not of the world any more than I am of the world. 15 My prayer is not that you take them out of the world but that you protect them from the evil one. 16 They are not of the world, even as I am not of it. 17 Sanctify them by the truth; your word is truth. 18 As you sent me into the world, I have sent them into the world. NIV

Why does the world hate the followers of Jesus?

_____

3.   John 15:19-22

Underline the phrases "the world hates you" and "if they persecuted me, they will persecute you."

19 If you belonged to the world, it would love you as its own. As it is, you do not belong to the world, but I have chosen you out of the world. That is why the world hates you. 20 Remember the words I spoke to you: 'No servant is greater than his master.' If they persecuted me, they will persecute you also. If they obeyed my teaching, they will obey yours also. 21 They will treat you this way because of my name, for they do not know the One who sent me. NIV

Why does the world hate those who follow Jesus? _____

Have you experienced this? _____

4.   1 Peter 4:4-5

In this passage, underline the phrase "former friends."

4 Of course, your former friends will be very surprised when you don't eagerly join them anymore in the wicked things they do, and they will laugh at you in contempt and scorn. 5 But just remember that they must face the Judge of all, living and dead; they will be punished for the way they have lived. TLB

What type of rejection/persecution will your former friends provide?

_____

_____

Did you experience this type of rejection when you quit partying? Swearing? Watching or listening to ungodly music, movies, videos or television shows? Getting high? Going to the bars? Living together? If so, explain how you dealt with it.

_____

_____

Who will everyone face? _____

5.   2 Timothy 3:12

Underline the phrase "everyone who wants to live a godly life." Circle the phrase "will be persecuted."

In fact, everyone who wants to live a godly life in Christ Jesus will be persecuted... NIV

If you live a godly Christian life, what can you expect? _____

When you live your life based upon God's Word you are going to get some flack! When you make decisions that are not popular or that make people feel uneasy about their own behavior, you will likely be rejected, despised, made fun of, excluded . . . persecuted!

Make a decision that when this type of rejection comes your way, you will rejoice and praise the Lord anyway.

Remember, You're Never Alone

When you are rejected or dissed because of your faith, be encouraged to know that you really are not alone. Jesus promises to be with you always. It takes courage to be a Christian, to be a witness for Jesus and to proclaim your faith to your family and friends. It hurts to be ostracized or overlooked because you are a Christian. Perhaps you experienced the reality of being persecuted for your faith when you were overlooked for a job promotion, cut from the sports team, or laughed at and gossiped about in the dorm, office or neighborhood. Perhaps the most painful form of rejection is when your own family persecutes you for your faith. In some cultures, when you become a Christian you are absolutely cut off and disowned by your family. Whether we are mocked, rejected and persecuted by our own family, close friends, co-workers or neighbors because of our Christian testimony and witness for Jesus Christ, we can find comfort knowing that God will never reject us. We are not alone, the Lord embraces us. Let's look at a few verses on this subject.

1.   Hebrews 13:5

Underline the word "never."

God has said, "Never will I leave you; never will I forsake you." NIV

Though others may reject, leave, forsake and persecute you, will Jesus ever leave or forsake you?

The last of all human freedoms is the ability to choose one's own attitude in any set of circumstances. Victor Frankl, Nazi Concentration Camp Survivor

2.   Matthew 10:32-33

Underline the words "confesses/confess" and "deny/denies."

Therefore whoever confesses Me before men, him I will also confess before My Father who is in heaven. 33 But whoever denies Me before men, him I will also deny before My Father who is in heaven. NKJV

If we acknowledge Jesus Christ, what will He do for us? _____

_____

Remember, when you confess your faith in Jesus to others, Jesus is listening.

3.   John 12:42-43

Underline the phrase "they loved the praise of men more than the praise of God."

42 Nevertheless even among the rulers many believed in Him, but because of the Pharisees they did not confess Him, lest they should be put out of the synagogue; 43 for they loved the praise of men more than the praise of God. NKJV

What did these people love? _____

Describe a time when you were faced with choosing either the "praise of God" or the "praise of men".

_____

_____

_____

3.   Matthew 28:18-20

Underline the phrase "I am with you always."

18 He told his disciples, "I have been given all authority in heaven and earth. 19 Therefore go and make disciples in all the nations, baptizing them into the name of the Father and of the Son and of the Holy Spirit, 20 and then teach these new disciples to obey all the commands I have given you; and be sure of this-that I am with you always, even to the end of the world." TLB

What did Jesus tell us to do? _____

What did He promise us? _____

Yes, as we preach the gospel we will face persecution, but Jesus promised to be with us always.

4.   Mark 6:2-6

Underline verse 4.

2 The next Sabbath he went to the synagogue to teach, and the people were astonished at his wisdom and his miracles because he was just a local man like themselves. "He's no better than we are," they said. "He's just a carpenter, Mary's boy, and a brother of James and Joseph, Judas and Simon. And his sisters live right here among us." And they were offended! 4 Then Jesus told them, "A prophet is honored everywhere except in his hometown and among his relatives and by his own family." 5 And because of their unbelief he couldn't do any mighty miracles among them except to place his hands on a few sick people and heal them. 6 And he could hardly accept the fact that they wouldn't believe in him. TLB

What did Jesus say about our relatives and family? _____

_____

&**Nugget**& Often because our family members are so personally acquainted with us, sometimes they have a hard time respecting or responding to us and our new life in Christ. It can be somewhat awkward. After all, they know our flaws and human weakness and they wonder, *"Who do you think you are?"* It's easy for family to feel that we are judging them, coming across in a self-righteous or holier-than-thou way, which of course is not our intent. Jesus was perfect and He was rejected by his own family and friends.

At times even our own family members will reject us because of our faith in Jesus Christ. Perhaps you have experienced this very thing. Jesus had some very strong words in Matthew 10:33-39, *"But if anyone denies me here on earth, I will deny that person before my Father in heaven. Don't imagine that I came to bring peace to the earth! No, I came to bring a sword. I have come to set a man against his father, and a daughter against her mother, and a daughter-in-law against her mother-in-law. Your enemies will be right in your own household! If you love your father or mother more than you love me, you are not worthy of being mine; or if you love your son or daughter more than me, you are not worthy of being mine. If you refuse to take up your cross and follow me, you are not worthy of being mine. If you cling to your life, you will lose it; but if you give it up for me, you will find it."* NLT It's a sad reality that sometimes your enemies will be right in your own household. Make a decision that when this type of rejection comes your way, you will choose to follow Jesus with your whole heart in the midst of the rejection, pain and heartbreak you may feel.

5.   Psalm 68:6

Underline the word "solitary."

God sets the solitary in families... NKJV

What does God do for the solitary? _____

_____

☙**Nugget**☙ This passage tells us that God sets the lonely or homeless in families, but I like to look at this passage in another way. When it says that "God sets the solitary in families" could it mean that if you are the first one to be born-again or saved in your family, that God sets you as an example and witness to the rest of your family? Does God set the solitary Christian in a family to be a light and beacon for Christ? Being the first person in your family to become a Christ follower is a wonderful and challenging position to be in. I know this from experience. Of course, it's wonderful to come into a personal relationship with Jesus and if you are the first one in your family to do so, you are blazing a trail for the rest of your family. You have the privilege, responsibility and challenge of being a witness for Christ, and as you are led by the Spirit, to do your best in leading your family to Christ.

6.   Proverbs 18:24

Underline the words "closer than a brother."

But there is a friend who sticks closer than a brother. NKJV

If your family rejects you, who will stick by you even closer than your brother?

_____

Persecution will come, but remember to rejoice and be glad knowing that Jesus will never leave you or forsake you!

Appreciate me now, avoid the rush. Anonymous

Scriptures To Chew On

Taking time to meditate on and memorize God's Word is invaluable. Hiding His Word in our hearts will strengthen us for the present and arm us for the future. Here are two verses to memorize and chew on this week. Write these verses on index cards and carry them with you this week. If you will post them in your bathroom, dashboard, desk, locker or other convenient places, you will find these Scriptures taking root in your heart.

"Yes, and all who desire to live godly in Christ Jesus will suffer persecution."
2 Timothy 3:12, NKJV

"But I say to you, love your enemies, bless those who curse you,
do good to those who hate you,
and pray for those who spitefully use you and persecute you…"
Matthew 5:44, NKJV

Group Discussion

1. Describe any situations you've faced where your faith in Jesus Christ has cost you and caused you to be rejected or overlooked.

2. Describe any situations where you didn't use wisdom and faced "persecution" or rejection for your faith that was not necessary. In other words, sometimes we don't use wisdom and good judgement and we bring a certain degree of persecution upon ourselves that is not necessary. Have you ever done that? If so, describe the experience.

3. Describe the way you've handled being persecuted by your family or close friends.

Personal Notes

The "Bite Sized Bible Study Series"
By Beth Jones

When your words came, I ate them;
they were my joy and my heart's delight . . .
Jeremiah 15:16 NIV

- Six practical Bible studies for Christians living in today's culture.
- Each book contains 6 sessions designed for individual & small group study.
- Great studies targeting men, women, believers and seekers of all ages.
- Convenient size 6" x 9", each book is between 80-144 pages.
- Fill-in-the-blank book with Group Discussion questions after each session.
- "Nuggets" throughout each study explain Scriptures in easy to follow way.
- Written in a contemporary style using practical illustrations.
- Perfect for small group curriculum, bookstores and churches.

Satisfied Lives For Desperate Housewives
God's Word On Proverbs 31
Great Study For Women, Retail $7.99
ISBN: 1-933433-04-3

Session 1: Desperate For God
Session 2: Desperate For Balance
Session 3: Desperate For A Good Marriage
Session 4: Desperate For Godly Kids
Session 5: Desperate To Serve
Session 6: Desperate For Purpose

Grace For The Pace
God's Word For Stressed & Overloaded Lives
Great Study For Men & Women, Retail $7.99
ISBN: 1-933433-02-7

Session 1: Escape From Hamsterville
Session 2: Help Is Here
Session 3: How Do You Spell Relief?
Session 4: Get A Bigger Frying Pan
Session 5: Houston, We Have A Problem!
Session 6: Time Keeps On Ticking

Call Or Go Online To Order:
800-596-0379
www.valleypresspublishers.com

Kissed Or Dissed

God's Word For Feeling Rejected & Overlooked
Great Study For Women, Retail $7.99
ISBN: 1-933433-01-9

Session 1: Dissed 101
Session 2: Blessed & Highly Favored
Session 3: Edit Your Life
Session 4: That's What I'm Talking About
Session 5: Sow Acceptance Seeds
Session 6: Just Like Jesus

What To Do When You Feel Blue

God's Word For Depression & Discouragement
Great Study For Men & Women, Retail $7.99
ISBN: 1-933433-00-0

Session 1: When The Sky Is Not Blue
Session 2: No Pity Parties Allowed
Session 3: The Things You Could Think
Session 4: Go To Your Happy Place
Session 5: You've Got To Have Friends
Session 6: Lift Up The Down

The Friends God Sends

God's Word On Friendship & Chick Chat
Great Study For Women, Retail $7.99
ISBN: 1-933433-05-1

Session 1: Friendship Realities
Session 2: The Friendship Workout
Session 3: God-Knit Friendships
Session 4: Who's On Your Boat?
Session 5: Anatomy Of A Friendship Famine
Session 6: A Friend Of God

Don't Factor Fear Here

God's Word For Overcoming Anxiety, Fear & Phobias
Great Study For Men & Women, Retail $7.99
ISBN: 1-933433-03-5

Session 1: Fear of Death
Session 2: Fear of Man
Session 3: Fear of Danger
Session 4: Fear of Change
Session 5: Fear Factors - Peace & Love
Session 6: Fear Factors - Faith & Courage

Why The Gory, Bloody Details?
By Beth Jones

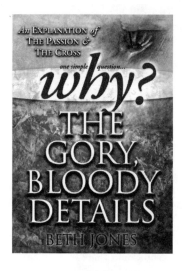

*. . . right before
your very eyes–
Jesus Christ
(the Messiah)
was openly
and graphically
set forth
and
portrayed
as crucified . . .
Galatians 3:1, AMP*

Why The Gory, Bloody Details?
An Explanation of the Passion and the Cross

Retail Paperback $4.99, Hardcover $7.99

ISBN: 0-9717156-6-1 Paperback
ISBN: 0-9717156-7-X Hardcover

This contagious 96 page giftbook answers the basic question, "Why did Jesus have to die on the cross?" People want to know: Why did Jesus endure such brutality? Why did God allow His own Son to be murdered? Why the gore and blood? It's a great evangelistic gift for unsaved friends and family and a great educational resource for believers who want to understand the cross and the passion.

- *Evangelistic gift book explains the cross—perfect for seekers.*
- *Gospel presented in a relevant, easy to understand way.*
- *Gift book size 4" x 6", 96 pages.*
- *Written in a contemporary style using practical illustrations.*
- *Hardcover and paperback.*

ALLEY PRESS
PUBLISHERS

A Ministry of Kalamazoo Valley Family Church
995 Romence Road
Portage, MI 49024
Ph. 800-596-0379
www.valleypresspublishers.com

Beth**Jones**.org

a
simple
casual
blog

articles
and
bible
studies

topics
like
eternal life
girl stuff
healing
ministry
finances
holy spirit
prayer
victory
faq

click
it

.